UNDERSTANDING

Gauguin

Barbara Hope Steinberg

An analysis of the work of the legendary
rebel artist of the 19th century

Self-portrait with a Halo
1889
Oil on panel
$31\frac{1}{4} \times 20\frac{1}{4}$ in
(79.4 × 51.4 cm)
National Gallery of Art,
Washington D.C.,
Chester Dale Collection

Published by A&W
VISUAL LIBRARY
New York and London
Originated, designed and
produced by Trewin
Copplestone Publishing
Ltd, London
© Trewin Copplestone
Publishing Ltd 1976

Filmset and
reproduced by
Photoprint Plates Ltd,
Rayleigh, Essex
Printed in Great Britain by
Chromoworks Ltd,
Nottingham

Library of Congress
Catalog Card Number:
75-37495
ISBN 0-89104-033-1

Gauguin: His Life and Times

The legend of Paul Gauguin is perhaps the most famous in art history: he was the man who abandoned civilization in middle age and fled to the tropics to paint. Like many legends, it is a great oversimplification.

Gauguin was born in Paris in 1848, during the Revolution. His father, Clovis, was a journalist, but it was his mother, Aline-Marie, and her family, who influenced Gauguin most. She was the daughter of the engraver, André Chazal, and Flora Tristan. Chazal tried to murder his wife, and was imprisoned. Flora was the illegitimate daughter of Thérèse Laisnay and a Spanish colonel of aristocratic family, Don Mariano de Tristan Moscoso. His family were wealthy and powerful Peruvian settlers; Gauguin believed that they had intermarried with Inca nobles. Certainly, Flora went to Peru; the book she wrote about her travels launched her on a literary career. Eventually she became a revolutionary social reformer. Gauguin worshipped her, and was profoundly affected by her romantic rebellion.

Emigrating to Peru with his family to escape the Revolution, Clovis died on the voyage. Aline and her children, however, stayed with powerful relatives in Lima until Gauguin was six. This life of ease in an exotic paradise haunted Gauguin, and he spent the rest of his life trying to return to his childhood Eden. As soon as possible, he attempted to escape from the dull misery of provincial France; from 1865 to 1871, he served in the merchant marine and French navy.

Portrait of Mette
1877
White marble
h. 13 in
(33 cm)
Courtauld Institute
Galleries,
London

Eventually, however, Gauguin's guardian, Gustave Arosa, got Gauguin a job on the Paris stock exchange. Gauguin settled down to a bourgeois life, marrying a Danish governess, Mette Gad, in 1873; she bore him five children. But Gauguin was already moving toward an artist's life when he married. He studied Arosa's fine collection of modern French paintings, and began painting under the tutelage of Arosa's daughter, Marguerite. By 1879, Gauguin himself was collecting art, primarily Impressionist work, and he worked with Camille Pissarro (1831-1903), who encouraged him greatly.

In 1882, French finance was in trouble. It seems as likely that Gauguin lost his job as that he resigned. By 1883, he had become a full-time painter. He moved to Rouen to be near Pissarro, and to live more cheaply. Mette, meanwhile, took the children to Copenhagen, where she supported them by teaching and translating. Gauguin joined them in 1884, but the year was not a success. He loathed her staid, middle-class family and friends, and did everything possible to offend them.

In 1886, Gauguin left Paris for Pont Aven, in Brittany. He fell in love with its primitive

A portrait of Flora Tristan
(1803-1844), Gauguin's
grandmother

Photograph taken at the
Pension Gloanec,
Pont-Aven of Gauguin and
his friends. Gauguin is
seated in the front row.

Camille Pissarro: *Gauguin
Carving the Little
Parisienne*
1880-81
Drawing
Nationalmuseum,
Stockholm

people and wild landscape; it was, indeed,
his first great step towards his rejection of
Western sophistication and civilization.
Continuing on this path, he went to Panama
in 1887. Sickness and poverty drove him
away from Martinique, where he had continued after Panama, but the visit bore fruit:
the brilliant colours and flat designs of his
new paintings marked a definitive departure
from Impressionism. In 1888, he returned to
Brittany, and soon consolidated his progress.
His paintings became solid, monumental,
and poetic. About this time, he became
friendly with Emile Bernard (1868-1941).
There was considerable argument between
them about who was actually responsible
for the stylistic revolution called *cloissonisme*,
in which flat, bright areas of colour were en-
closed by dark lines. It seems likely that
Bernard originated it, but Gauguin took the
idea much further.

It must be observed that Gauguin was
always incapable of treating friends as
equals. He insisted on dominating Bernard
and Schuffenecker, another painter, and
later, the artists Meyer de Haan and Séru-
sier. His disciples gave him enormous psy-
chological and financial support, but when

they finally rebelled, Gauguin was furious. Nowhere is this more evident than in his relationship with Van Gogh.

In 1888, primarily to please Theo Van Gogh (an art dealer who might help him), Gauguin stayed with Vincent Van Gogh in Arles for ten weeks. There was unremitting tension between them. Van Gogh wanted an artistic fraternity, but Gauguin insisted on being the master. Van Gogh gladly became his pupil, but the concepts that Gauguin forced on him—the rejection of naturalism and working abstractly from memory—were totally alien. This conflict stimulated Gauguin, but drove Van Gogh over the brink to madness. After attacking Gauguin,

Section of a letter to an unknown collector c. 1896
10×9½ in (25.4×24 cm)
Mr and Mrs Alex M. Lewyt Collection, New York

Bonjour Monsieur Gauguin
1889
36½×29 in
(113×92 cm)
National Gallery,
Prague

Self-portrait for Van Gogh
1888
Oil on canvas
17¾×21⅝ in
(44.1×54.8 cm)
Rijksmuseum
Vincent Van Gogh,
Amsterdam

4

And the Gold of their Bodies
1901
Oil on canvas
26⅜ × 29⅞ in
(67 × 75.9 cm)
Musée du Louvre,
Paris

he cut off his own earlobe and sent it to a prostitute. Gauguin notified Theo and returned to Paris.

In 1889, Gauguin went back to Brittany, going from Port Aven to the more remote Le Pouldu. By this time, he was the acknowledged master there, with a growing reputation. His fame spread, and by late 1890, he was in close touch with the Symbolist writers. Yet, perversely, he abandoned this possibility of French success to go to Tahiti in 1891.

With the official status of an artist on an unpaid mission, Gauguin embarked on his greatest adventure. After his arrival he soon moved from Papeete to Mataiea, seeking the real Tahiti of his dreams. He took a Tahitian wife, Teha'amana, and lived like a native. But the old Tahitian culture was gone; Tahiti was now merely a poor French colony. Disappointed, and increasingly ill with syphilis, Gauguin was eventually repatriated to France in 1893. Despite his physical and mental torment, his stay in Tahiti changed his life and marked him forever. His vision triumphed over reality, and gave birth to rich, golden paintings in which he celebrated the carefree existence and primitive splendour of his dreams.

In Paris, Gauguin found himself out of touch. He was distant, withdrawn, and arrogant. He dressed flamboyantly, decorated his apartment exotically, and took a foreign mistress, Annah, the (alleged) Javanese. In 1894, he went to Pont Aven. In a fight with some sailors over Annah, he broke his leg. While he was bedridden, Annah sacked his studio and left him.

Embittered, Gauguin left France forever, and returned to Tahiti in 1895. He settled at Punaauia with a new mistress, Pahura, until 1901. Bedevilled by conjunctivitis and the syphilis which would kill him, crippled by his bad leg, and desperately poor, he alternated between happiness and misery. In 1897, disasters multiplied: his favourite daughter, Aline, died, precipitating the final break with Mette; he had to move, and he became much sicker. Eventually, he attempted suicide, but failed.

In 1901, Gauguin moved to the more primitive Marquesas Islands, still in search of his dream. For much of his last five years, he did not paint a lot, but worked as a draughtsman and journalist. Yet, despite the horror of this time, he produced during these years some of his finest paintings – radiant, lyrical, and mysterious. In 1903, Gauguin died. The paradise he never really found in life now exists forever, immortalized in his art. By sacrificing family, friends, and life itself, Paul Gauguin did return to Eden.

5

Technique

The Seaweed Harvesters
1889
Oil
No measurements available
Folkwang Museum,
Essen

Detail of the seated woman from *The Seaweed Harvesters*

Gauguin has long been acknowledged to be one of the most flamboyant rebels in the history of art. Despite this, his painting technique seems to have developed in much the same way as that of the vast majority of Western artists, however revolutionary or conservative they may otherwise have been. The artist, when a child, paints freely and inventively, without any technical restraints or inhibitions. As he becomes more aware of his talent, he attempts to achieve a more disciplined, tighter realism, usually with a high degree of finish. He will then be influenced by artists slightly older then himself, and will apply paint in their manner. Only then will he gradually develop his own style and his own technique.

So it was with Gauguin. Even in his very early flirtation with realism, he was influenced by Impressionism. Soon he fell completely

Detail from *Barbaric Tales*

Barbaric Tales 1902 Oil on canvas 51⅛ × 36 in (129.9 × 91.4 cm) Folkwang Museum, Essen

under the spell of the Impressionists, and for some time painted in the Impressionist style: loosely, in small blobs and flecks, following the direction of each form. This created a rich, lively surface of vibrating colours.

Eventually, however, Gauguin became dissatisfied with Impressionism. In discarding the Impressionist conception of the artist as an eye recording nature, he also cast off his Impressionist technique. In developing his own technique, Gauguin followed yet another classic path in art history.

There has always been a dichotomy between artists who emphasize line, and those who emphasize colour. The former usually apply paint thinly, keeping the surface flat, while the colourists use thick, juicy impastos, enlivened by exciting brush work. Though Gauguin was a fine colourist – indeed, sometimes a brilliant one – the essential nature of his work was linear. Hence, he kept the actual

paint thin and flat, however vivid and intense the colour. Fortunately, necessity accompanied invention in his case, since he could not afford much paint, particularly towards the end of his life.

Gauguin's work was always controlled and carefully conceived; there was nothing of the wild man in his technique. In one aspect, however, it did show his rebellious nature, his eagerness to experiment: Gauguin would paint on almost anything. Coarse canvas, paper, wood, glass, silk, doors, walls, and windows all provided adequate surfaces for his work. Because the paint was so very thin, the surface below almost always showed through it, and he more often than not exposed these unusual surfaces deliberately.

Both paintings on these pages are characteristic of Gauguin's mature technique. In the earlier painting, *The Seaweed Harvesters,* we see the paint applied in long, parallel strokes, following the contours of each form. These strokes are built into simplified shapes, with little variation of colour within each shape. Broad contour lines enclose each shape. This combination of emphatic line, simplified shapes, and paint applied thinly with little change in the direction or length of strokes, makes a flat, bold pattern.

The same is true of the later *Barbaric Tales,* but here the surface is developed with greater subtlety. The contour lines are not so harsh; sometimes they are omitted. There is greater variation in the colours and strokes within each shape, but less extreme contrasts between colours. There is an airy, atmospheric quality in much of the brushwork, and it is a warm, mellow, and unified vision.

Use of Colour

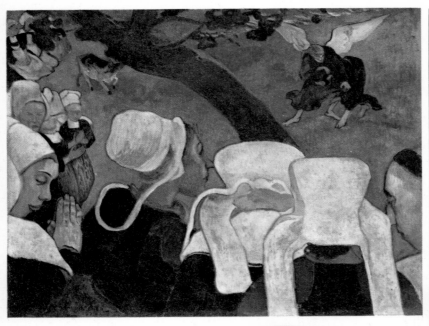

The Vision after the Sermon
1888
Oil on canvas
28¾ × 36¼ in
(73 × 92.1 cm)
National Gallery of
Scotland,
Edinburgh

Detail of Jacob and the
Angel from *The Vision after
the Sermon*

realistic colour entirely. Colour became, for Gauguin, a totally imaginative conception. He used it to create a mood, to charge a painting with emotion, and to establish a complex, intricate, ambiguous symbolism.

In one of Gauguin's mature works, *The Vision after the Sermon* on this page, we see a powerful embodiment of this revolutionary use of colour. The painting depicts a group of Breton villagers departing from church. Under the influence of the sermon they have just heard, they see a vision of Jacob wrestling with the Angel. The villagers themselves are painted in dull, sombre hues, colours close to those of reality, without being totally realistic. They are, in fact, simplified and subdued to form the greatest possible contrast with the rest of the painting. So, too,

Gauguin was one of the most adventurous and inventive colourists in modern painting. He extended the role of colour far beyond the boundaries fixed by tradition into completely new territory. Most artists have used colour, however carefully composed, primarily to reproduce the colours seen in nature; so, too, did Gauguin, at first. In his early Impressionist works, he used flickering strokes of colour to capture the effect of the many colours, lights, and shadows he saw in each object. Gradually, he simplified this, painting each mass in the one colour which seemed to dominate it. Eventually, he eschewed the tree and the upper ground of the painting are painted in relatively realistic browns and greens. But the vision itself is rendered in literally visionary colours. The ground on which the struggle takes place is a brilliant scarlet; the flesh of the combatants is alight with yellow and orange; the Angel's hair is like flame, his wings are golden fires. These luminous colours are reflected on the face and neck of one of the villagers, linking the visionaries and the vision. Gauguin often likened colour to music, and he did indeed orchestrate this composition. The colours of the villagers are like the dull tolling of a church bell, while those of the vision are the clear, shrill cry of a heavenly trumpet.

Such extreme colour contrasts are typical of much of Gauguin's earlier mature work. In his later work, however, the colour became more subtle and unified without losing any of its potency. Indeed, this very subtlety gave his paintings a greater power and monumentality. In *Nevermore*, we can see how this was achieved. The girl's body glows with the orange, green, yellow, and umber of rich bronze. It seems to reflect the light from her yellow pillow and from the

darting whites, blue-greens, and crimson of the cloth beneath her. The rest of the colours of the room echo these in hushed, darkened tones, while the sky and trees beyond come alight again in a strange violet and rose night. By keeping his colours close to each other in hue, Gauguin binds the elements in a mysterious grandeur. No longer shrill, the colour now resounds in rich harmonies.

Detail of the bird from
Nevermore

Nevermore
1897
Oil on canvas
$23\frac{3}{8} \times 45\frac{5}{8}$ in
(59.4×115.8 cm)
Courtauld Institute
Galleries,
London

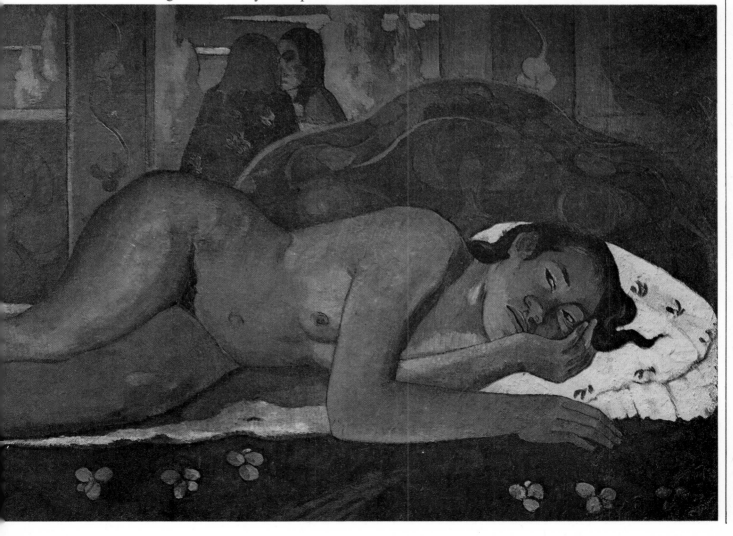

Prints and Drawings

Noa Noa
1894
Woodcut
Musée du Louvre,
Paris

Considering his position in art history, Gauguin said, 'You have known for a long time what I wanted to establish; the *right* to dare everything . . . The public owes me nothing, since my pictorial work is only *relatively* good, but the painters who, today, are profiting from this freedom, do owe me something'. We may disagree with Gauguin's opinion of his work, but about his influence, he was entirely correct. He was devoted to experimentation, and nowhere is this more obvious than in his drawings and prints.

In drawing, Gauguin experimented with many media and with highly individual and strange imagery. An outstanding example of this is the *Portrait of Jean Moréas* on the next page. Moréas published the Symbolist Manifesto, and this drawing is itself a Symbolist manifesto, as Gauguin indicated on the scroll reading 'Soyez Symboliste'. Technically, it is almost deliberately crude, but very forceful. The strong, simplified, exaggerated head reflects Gauguin's interest in caricature. In combination with the peacock and the cherub bearing a laurel sprig, it becomes almost funny and rather theatrical. But, beyond humour, this is a rather perplexing

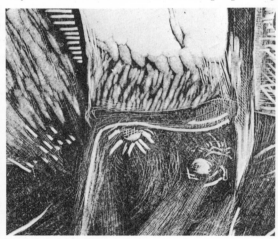

Detail from *Noa Noa*

Detail from *Nave Nave Fenua*

10

Soyez Symboliste—Portrait of Jean Moréas
1891
Pen, brush and ink
13⅞ × 16⅝ in
(35 × 42 cm)
Present owner unknown

Nave Nave Fenua
(Land of Sensuous Pleasure)
1894
Woodcut
14 × 8 in
(35.6 × 20.3 cm)
Courtauld Institute
Galleries, London

combination of images. While we cannot ascribe any exact meaning to them, they carry powerful connotations of pride and a vigour that unites style and imagery.

This curious complexity and technical and stylistic adventurousness are carried still further in the woodcuts *Noa Noa* and *Nave Nave Fenua* (Land of Sensuous Pleasure). In the 19th century, the woodcut as a medium for original art had fallen into almost total disuse, and served largely as a vehicle for slick and facile reproduction. Gauguin was one of the prime begetters of its renaissance. He recognized no technical limitations, and we can see many of his innovations in these prints. Every possible texture is employed. Fine scratches create grey areas, bold scratches are drawn coarsely, making jagged patterns, and the foliage seems to be drawn out of the wood, and shares its nature. Often Gauguin draws white lines into black, surprising us by this reversal. In *Nave Nave Fenua* all of these textures intensify the mystery of this strange image. A peculiar lizard creature darts toward a voluptuous Tahitian Eve; the exotic foliage is threatening and spiky; the space is undefined and shifting, framed on one side by curious signs. We are in Gauguin's oddly uneasy, yet enchanted paradise.

Composition:
Faa Iheihe

Faa Iheihe
(Decoration)
1898
Oil on canvas
$21\frac{1}{4} \times 66\frac{3}{4}$ in
(54×169.5 cm)
Tate Gallery,
London

Detail of the central figure
from *Faa Iheihe*

From quite early in his career, Gauguin showed a great interest in experimenting with composition. He was, indeed, confronted by unusual problems, working as he did entirely from imagination. It is, after all, one thing to paint an imaginary figure; it is quite another to imagine an entire world, and compose it so that it becomes convincing. Gauguin had not only to create a different race of people; he had also to create a new kind of space in which they could exist.

It is not surprising, therefore, that Gauguin drew inspiration from many different sources to help him in this task. Almost all of these sources were non-Western. Like the Impressionists, he was at first greatly influenced by the Japanese print. A significant example of this is *The Vision after the Sermon*, which was discussed on pages 8-9. The entire composition is asymmetric: a tree strikes a bold

diagonal across it, and the villagers are massed diagonally from corner to corner across the lefthand side. In the upper right, the figures of the vision are isolated. The scarlet plane on which they wrestle occupies a vast space of the canvas, and this plane is tilted up towards us, making the entire composition very flat. At the same time, the great disparity in size between the villagers and Jacob and the Angel seems to contradict this flatness, implying, as it does, an enormous distance between the two groups. The edges of the canvas slice arbitrarily through the figures of the villagers, emphasizing still more the isolation of the only two complete figures, the figures of the vision. All of these devices—the strong diagonals, the enormous shifts of scale and contrasts in colour—create a composition which is at once exciting and alive, yet flat and decorative.

As Gauguin's style developed, his compositions, like the other aspects of his art, became more subtle and intricate. Increasingly he drew on other sources, one of the primary ones being the relief sculptures from a Javanese temple. From these sculptures he learned to combine many figures in a long frieze. He learned, too, paradoxically to contain solid figures within a shallow, almost flat, space. Both of these lessons are obvious in *Faa Iheihe* (Decoration), on this page. *Faa Iheihe* has two dominant directions of movement. The painting as a whole is a frieze which moves horizontally through a shallow space parallel to the picture plane. Figures, trees, vines, and passages of pure colour penetrate that space in a series of verticals.

Detail of the left-hand group from *Faa Iheihe*

They are, indeed, like irregular musical intervals. Some, like the trees, are swift and straight, while the vines curve sinuously at a slower pace. The figures are solid, almost stopping the eye, while the passages of pure colour flow gradually upwards. From Eastern and Egyptian sculpture, Gauguin learned the vocabulary of static, hieratic gestures and poses which he employs here. The figures present themselves to us in a still, formal ritual. The colour throughout is warm and intense. Since the intensity is equal in every area of the canvas, it flattens the space still further. Again, there are irrational changes in the size of the figures. Irrational, too, is the space, which floats around and behind the figures, providing no real ground or horizon. It is the space of dreams, rhythmic, flowing, and luminous, in a silent dream of paradise.

Gauguin's Symbolism

Human Anguish
(Vintage at Arles)
1888
Oil on canvas
No measurements available
Ordrupgaard Museum,
Copenhagen,
Wilhelm Hansen Collection

Detail of standing figure from *Human Anguish*

All of Gauguin's mature work was influenced by the ideas of Symbolist writers, the *avant-garde* of French literature at that time. Rebelling against materialism and the concomitant naturalism in art, the Symbolists turned away from nature to the imagination, seeking the springs of creativity in the inner self. Gauguin said, 'Do not copy too much from nature. Art is an abstraction. Draw it forth from nature by dreaming in front of her, and think more of creation than the actual result. The only way to reach God is to do what he does: create . . .'

Unlike many Symbolist artists, however, Gauguin never painted allegories. No single image in his work was intended to correspond strictly to an idea or emotion. Rather, he sought to create a synthesis of all aspects of

his art—lines, colours, forms, images—and with this synthesis to evoke an all-pervasive poetry and mystery. As he said, 'In painting, one must search rather for suggestion than for description, as is done in music . . . I obtain by an arrangement of lines and colours, with the pretext of some sort of subject taken from life or from nature, symphonies, harmonies which represent nothing absolutely real in the vulgar sense of the word, which express directly no idea, but which provoke thoughts as music provokes thoughts, without the help of ideas or images, simply through the mysterious relationships which exist between our brains and these arrangements of lines and colours'.

Though we cannot, therefore, ascribe any absolute meaning to any of Gauguin's images, we can see in them poetic metaphors for aspects of the human condition. In *Human Anguish* Gauguin uses a scene of the vintage to conjure up a sense of intense misery and exhaustion. The bending figures in the back are depersonalized; their pose embodies the tiring repetition of unremitting labour. The sombre figure on the left is drained of life and vitality. But these figures, and all the lines of the composition, serve to focus our concentration on the seated figure. Coarsened and brutalized by toil, her face almost a macabre mask, she hunches forward, an image of bitterness and defeat.

By the time he painted *D'où Venons-Nous? Que Sommes-Nous? Où Allons-Nous?*, Gauguin had evolved a more complex and ambiguous symbolism. This picture was painted as his last will and testament before his suicide attempt, and, as its title suggests, it was a statement of his philosophy. It is a painting of profound contrasts and paradoxes. Intended to be read from right to left, it goes from birth, with women grouped around a baby, through the concerns of adult life, to death, closing with the resigned figure of an old woman, whose pose repeats that of the central figure in *Human Anguish*. All of these images suggest meanings: An idol conjures up the mysteries of religion, in which two figures seem absorbed. Significantly, the central figure plucks an apple from a tree. Is it the Tree of Life or of Knowledge? This is paradise, but after the Fall of Man. Despite its exotic luxuriance and voluptuous sexuality, it is shadowed. The sombre harmonies and solemn figures convey a mood of profound pessimism. We are left with the question: Whence do we come? What are we? Where are we going?

Details of *D'où Venons-Nous? Que Sommes-Nous? Où Allons-Nous?*
(see pages 16-17)

D'où Venons-Nous? Que
Sommes-Nous? Où Allons-
Nous? (Whence do we come?
What are we? Where are we
going?)
1897
Oil on canvas
54¾ × 147½ in
(139.1 × 374.9 cm)
Museum of Fine Arts, Boston
Arthur Gordon Tompkins Collection

Drawings of Brittany

Drawing is the most private part of an artist's work; it is in drawing that he thinks and learns, feeling his way on paper. Gauguin, otherwise public to the point of flamboyance, regarded drawing in this way. He was not a facile draftsman, and indeed, abhorred facility and academically scientific draftsmanship. Rather, he worked slowly over his drawings, labouring to capture the essential character of a figure in a few simple, assured lines and strongly defined masses. It was almost always the figure, because figures were the most important element in his mature work. Unlike many artists, Gauguin rarely made studies for entire composi-

tions. He did, however, make studies of individual figures for paintings and he reused poses constantly; a single figure may appear in several paintings, assuming a different meaning in each. The most important single influence on these drawings was Edgar Degas (1834-1917), arguably the greatest draftsman of his time. Gauguin often copied poses from Degas's figures, seeking the same sure knowledge and boldness.

All three drawings on these pages are studies for paintings, and all are of figures in poses adapted from Degas's work. Likewise, all were done in Brittany, and mark the beginning of Gauguin's artistic maturity.

Brittany had a profound effect on him. He loved the primitive simplicity and coarse power of its landscape and inhabitants. These characteristics are captured in the drawings. In the *Study of a Breton Gleaner*, we see a peasant woman in Breton dress bent over her labour. The pose emphasizes the slow, literally back-breaking nature of the work. A few broad strokes of the chalk summarize the solid masses in sharp contrasts of dark and light, while a jagged, black line accentuates the contour of back, arm, and hand, drawing our attention to those parts most vitally engaged in the act of gleaning. All detail is omitted, leaving us simply the picture of a single strong gesture, frozen in time.

This same omission of irrelevant detail is noticeable in the *Study of a Female Bather*. Here, the masses are even less defined, only a few light strokes serving to indicate the solid shapes of the figure. Gauguin considered the contour line the most important thing in drawing, and here we can see it in almost pure form. It is stressed further because Gauguin re-used this drawing often, each time re-drawing the contour. It is a very different line from that which we saw in the *Gleaner*. Far from being jagged and angular, it is sinuous and graceful, emphasizing the rounded, sensuous curves of the body. Gauguin thus uses his line to capture the arabesques of pleasure, where before he had used it to explore the angles of toil.

In the *Study for a Woman in the Hay*, Gauguin again investigated the rhythms of work, but with a greater degree of complexity. While the contour line again emphasizes the rounded forms of the body, they are not sensuous, but coarse and muscular. Indeed, with a minimum of detail, all the muscles and bone structure are described much more explicitly, making the figure seem heavy, mannish, and almost brutalized. There is nothing seductive about that thick back, those work-hardened arms, or the pendulous breast. Rather, this is an objective picture of a woman almost transformed into an animal by work which demands everything of the body, but nothing of the mind.

Study of a Female Bather
1886
Coloured chalks
$22\frac{1}{2} \times 13\frac{1}{2}$ in
$(57.2 \times 34.5$ cm)
The Art Institute of Chicago
(Given in memory of
Charles B. Goodspeed and
Mrs Gilbert W. Chapman)

Study for a Woman in the Hay
1889
Charcoal and watercolour
$10\frac{1}{4} \times 15\frac{3}{4}$ in
$(26.3 \times 40$ cm)
Rijksmuseum
Vincent Van Gogh,
Amsterdam

19

Paintings of Brittany

Brittany's great effect on Gauguin cannot be emphasized too much. It was there that he found his first spiritual homeland and came of age artistically. Describing this, he said, 'I love Brittany: there I find the wild and primitive. When my wooden shoes ring on this stony soil, I hear the muffled, dull and mighty tone I am seeking in painting.'

Gauguin seemed to draw strength from that stony soil, and this strength gave a new vigour and originality to his painting. We see this manifested in *La Belle Angèle*, opposite. It is a portrait of a local Breton woman, but very different from any traditional portrait. The composition is divided into two sections, the formal, stylized portrait being contained in a semi-circle on the right. Gauguin uses the traditional Breton dress to form an almost abstract pattern of bold, flat shapes, with smaller decorative patterns contained within them. The triangular shapes of the red dress and white yoke draw our eye upwards to the face, while the wide black sleeves, white epaulets, and geometric head-dress repeat this rhythm. Indeed, the entire costume is a kind of frame around the face, which is itself simplified into a series of sharp angles and planes, looking more like stone than flesh. Paradoxically, the colour is warm and intense; each colour in the face is pure and high-pitched.

The other section of the composition echoes, emphasizes, and amplifies the portrait. The blue background is the same, but across it are scattered flowers and leaves, creating a light, airy pattern and mitigating the sternness of the portrait. The glowing orange of the lower section picks up the warm notes scattered in the portrait. Most curious is the Peruvian idol, which seems almost to duplicate the pose, shape and expression of the sitter. Perhaps this was Gauguin's witty reference to the 'primitive' character of Brittany. This painting shows the Symbolist influence on Gauguin, in its combination of disparate elements which form a mysterious but satisfying whole.

But 'the muffled, dull and mighty tone' resounds with even more grandeur in *The Green Christ*. Reversing the traditional order, Gauguin places the foreground in deep shadow and lets gentle light flow over the background. But there are no sharp contrasts; rather, the dark sea and sombre, cloud-strewn sky echo the sober hues in the foreground. The entire composition is simple and monumental, almost static. Gauguin achieves this by balancing the horizontal lines of sea and hilltop against the verticals of the cross, the left hand figure, and the hillside, forming a series of right angles. Against the prevailing calm, the gestures of Christ and the Breton woman become almost shocking. The characteristic contour line distinguishes the foreground group from the background, while the Breton woman's colouring unites her more with the landscape than with the stone figures. By these intricate means, Gauguin creates a deeply

The Green Christ
(The Breton Calvary)
1889
Oil on canvas
36¼ × 29 in
(92.1 × 73.7 cm)
Musées Royaux des
Beaux-Arts,
Brussels

LA BELLE ANGÈLE

La Belle Angèle
1889
Oil on canvas
$36\frac{1}{4} \times 28\frac{1}{2}$ in
(92.1×72.4 cm)
Musée du Louvre,
Paris

religious painting, uniting this Breton peasant both with the countryside and the mourning at Calvary, in which she participates. She becomes not only a fourth Mary, but a reflection of Christ, mirroring the angle of his pose, and significantly, tending a lamb. Gauguin was not a believing Christian, but was moved by the Bretons' deep belief. Inspired by a Romanesque sculpture at nearby Nizon, he has joined in this picture the figures of Calvary with the Breton world, illuminating the strong bond between them.

21

Drawings of Tahiti

Studies of Tahitian Women
*c.*1892
Pen and watercolour
$7\frac{1}{4} \times 10\frac{1}{4}$ in
(18.5×26 cm)
Musée du Louvre,
Paris

Gauguin spent his life searching for Paradise – a free, wild, primitive place, divorced from what he thought of as the unredeemably rotten civilization of the West, a place where the sun always shone and happiness was everlasting. The closest he came to that idea of Paradise was Tahiti. Everything about the place obsessed him: its warm colours, its exotic landscape, and most of all, its people. He drew and painted them constantly, trying to capture their poetry and mystery. The experience conferred a greater subtlety and freedom on his work than he had ever achieved before.

In the *Studies of Tahitian Women* on this page, we can see this new freedom already present shortly after he had arrived in Tahiti. His technique is looser and more delicate, but at the same time, he had lost none of his discipline, none of his concentration on capturing the essential nature of each figure, primarily through emphasis on the contour line. While the figures are drawn in poses which seem natural, it is significant that Gauguin seems to have found in these Tahi-

tian women exactly what he wanted to find. The women on the left stand in precisely the sort of static, hieratic posture that Gauguin admired in Egyptian art; the figure on the right assumes the pose of a statue of Dionysus of which Gauguin had a photograph. This alone indicates that Gauguin's Tahitian experience was more complex than it at first seems; his conception of Tahiti as Paradise was as much a creation of his imagination as a reality he discovered. Indeed, it is no accident that he chose Dionysus, with all its connotations of pagan abandon, as a model for this figure, which was to appear in several paintings. Transformed into a mysterious Polynesian being, it is a perfect symbol of the mixture of vastly different, yet related elements in Gauguin's peculiar chemistry.

This process is repeated in *Te Arii Vahine* (Queen of Beauty), again a study for a painting – one of the rare studies in which Gauguin worked out a complete composition as opposed to his usual practice of taking a single figure from a proposed composition.

For this 'Queen of Beauty', Gauguin used his young Tahitian mistress as a model, but had her take the pose of Edouard Manet's (1832-83) *Olympia*, which he had once copied. Thus, from Western art and Polynesian life, he created an image which was totally his own. It is in fact a dream, a dream of an exotic, luxuriant Eden, peopled by silent, mysterious figures, and ruled over by a nubile yet majestic queen. Against a loosely drawn landscape, her strong outlines make her stand out and emphasize the arrogant indolence of her pose. She is an idol of sensuality in a Golden Age, which perhaps achieved its perfect reality only in Gauguin's mind.

But Gauguin knew there was a dark side to life, even in Eden, and he embodied it in the drawing of *The Nightmare* that we illustrate here. Again, he took the Tahitian Eve and the figure on horseback from his previous work and placed them in a new context, with a new meaning. The result is a triumph. Surely, it must be this youthful, frightened Tahitian Eve, who is having the nightmare. Only her body, characteristically stocky, is given solidity, defined by bright light and Gauguin's vigorous line. The other ominous figures emerge only partially from shadowy caverns. The only explicit symbol is the serpent, an evil harbinger in Eden. One cannot ascribe an exact meaning to this Symbolist work, but its strange poetry haunts one like a dark presence.

The Nightmare
c. 1901
Monotype
Size unknown
Private Collection,
New York

Te Arii Vahine
(Queen of Beauty)
1896
Watercolour
6¾ × 9 in
(17.2 × 22.9 cm)
Mr and Mrs Ward Cheney
Collection,
New York

Paintings of Tahiti

Parau Parau
(Conversation)
1892
Medium not known
30×37¾ in
(76.2×95.9 cm)
Mr and Mrs John Hay
Whitney Collection,
New York

In Tahiti, Gauguin not only found the paradise of which he had dreamt since childhood, but ripened into his full artistic maturity. With Polynesia acting as a catalyst, both the form and content of his work underwent great changes. These changes are most noticeable in Gauguin's imagery, which was drawn almost totally from the island's people and landscape. But there were formal changes, too. The sun which drenched Tahiti saturated Gauguin's colours, which soon took on a glowing sonorousness. Warmth suffuses the characteristic gold, rose, umber, and green, and even creeps into the violet shadows. The lines and contrasts are less harsh; rather, a more subtle and mellow unity pervades his canvases.

We can see these changes in all the paintings on these pages. *Parau Parau* (Conversation), for example, is a typical scene of daily life in Tahiti. As we have seen in Gauguin's drawings, this appearance can be deceptive. The stylized pose of the girl on the left was taken from Javanese sculpture, while the circle of women was lifted from one of Gauguin's previous paintings. It is significant, too, that work, often a theme in his earlier canvases, is almost never present in Gauguin's Tahitian paintings. It seems unlikely that the Tahitian found it unnecessary to work at all, but in Gauguin's imagination

Nafea Faaipoipo (When are you to be married?) 1892
Medium unavailable 41¼ × 30½ in (104.8 × 77.5 cm)
Kunstmuseum, Basle, Staechelin Collection

they appeared as the golden people of a Golden Age, indolent and carefree. This is embodied in *Parau Parau*, in which voluptuous figures converse lazily in a luxuriant tropical landscape. This sensuous ease is echoed and emphasized by the composition and colour. The composition has become much looser and less contrived, while there is a similar freedom in the brushwork. Rich greens, dappled by yellow sunlight, dominate the painting; through the centre flows a rosy orange, which is repeated in smaller notes throughout the canvas. These colours create a warm harmony, which envelops the figures and the landscape in a pervasive peace.

Still another typical Tahitian scene is described in *Nafea Faaipoipo* (When are you to be married?). In this, our attention is focussed on the two girls, stocky, golden-brown, and beautiful. Their bodies are solid, sculptural, and monumental; at the same time, both they and the landscape are simplified into broad areas, combining to form a predominantly flat, decorative pattern. This flatness is emphasized by the colour: dominated again by the characteristic red, pink, gold, umber, and green, it is high-pitched, sunny, and intense; but because the intensity is equal throughout the painting, no single area advances or recedes. The composition is again more casual and less artificial, suiting the gentle harmony of daily life that Gauguin was trying to depict. Yet there is a certain ambiguity present. Gauguin himself used the word 'enigmatic' to describe the Tahitians, and it is apposite. The faces of these girls do not reveal anything; they and their landscape, for all the obvious joy Gauguin took in them, are being observed by an outsider.

In *Ta Matete* (The Market), a Tahitian market scene, the seated prostitutes are painted characteristically in the formalized postures of Egyptian art, making a horizontal frieze. The space is made still more shallow by the flatness of the broad areas of colour. These are predominantly warm and low-keyed; a few bright areas are woven into the decorative pattern, harmonizing rather than contrasting, like shapes in an Oriental carpet. This combination of stylization and flatness transforms a casual scene of daily life into a mysterious, formal tapestry.

Detail from *Ta Matete* (The Market) 1892 Oil on canvas
28¾ × 36¼ in (73 × 92.1 cm)
Kunstmuseum, Basle

Sculpture and Ceramics

Oviri
c. 1894-5
Stoneware, partially glazed
h. 28¾ in
(73 cm)
Private Collection,
Paris

It seems almost inevitable that Gauguin, who loved experimenting with many media, would also experiment with sculpture. His attitude towards it, however, was paradoxical. In ceramics, he began by making pottery, but soon pushed through traditional boundaries and turned his pots into sculpture. Conversely, in wood he always preferred carving relief to making sculpture in the round. In both, he used the rich earth colours and golds often found in his painting. He had, in fact, a painter's conception of sculpture, emphasizing line, colour, and surface decoration, rather than creating three-dimensional form. Yet, at the same time, he had the modern sculptor's great respect for the character of each medium. Consequently, he preferred to make hand-coiled pots rather than use the wheel, which he considered mechanical, and he searched for the forms and colours inherent in clay. In his wood sculpture, he emphasized the grain of the medium and the forms and textures that came naturally from the use of the chisel. We can see the results of this highly individual attitude in the sculptures on these pages.

The *Self-portrait Jug* was undoubtedly influenced by Peruvian portrait pots. Gauguin transformed the simple jug into sculp-

Soyez Mysterieuses 1890 Wood relief
Madame Alban d'Andoque de Seriège Collection, Beziers

ture, modelling the clay to achieve the flickering, lively surface found in much of the best 19th-century French work. This strong, brooding, sombre head is very far from being purely decorative, and embodies Gauguin's tormented introspection at the time. Characteristically, it is made in stoneware, for which Gauguin had an almost mystical respect. He seems to have seen in the toughness and deep, warm colour obtained after high firing, a metaphysical analogy for the emotions he wanted to express. Describing this, Félix Fenéon said, 'Stoneware, spurned by all, funereal and hard, he loves it . . .'

But it was wood that Gauguin loved most, and from which he made one of his sculptural masterpieces, *Soyez Amoureuses et Vous Serez Heureuses* (Be loving and you will be happy). One can see in this work many of the attributes characteristic of both his painting and sculpture: the intricate symbolism, the emphasis on line and glowing, earthy colour, the irrational, subjective changes in the size of figures, and the shallow, ambiguous space. This space is flattened still further by Gauguin's technique of carving the entire relief at the same depth, making no concessions to illusion. The result is one of his most curious, complex works.

The title, *Soyez Armoureuses et Vous Serez Heureuses*, is made prominent in the design, and seems to declare Gauguin's philosophy, yet everything else in the relief contradicts it. The voluptuous mulatto, significantly wearing a wedding ring, is terrified at being grasped by Gauguin himself, portrayed as a monster. This portrayal of himself shows a defeated, withdrawn, yet defiantly childlike man. The region towards which he draws the woman is inhabited by a primitive idol of Woman and a crouching ram. An unattractive and long-nosed person peers over a wall, spying disapprovingly on lovers. There is, in fact, no promise of happiness at all in the entire composition–only barbaric fears, primitive lusts, bitterness and brutality. Perhaps we may find the key in the flowering tree and the fox. The tree is a symbol of fertility, while the fox, who stares out at us, is the Indian symbol of perversity. Gauguin seems to have identified with the fox, and he may thus have been referring

ironically to his own perversity in advocating love–the love which he, rejected and unhappy, had been refused, and could not give.

The relief *Soyez Mysterieuses* is also carved largely in two-dimensional terms, more drawn than modelled with the chisel. Moreover, the carving is crude and brutal. But the crudity and flatness emphasize the sensuous nature of the woman's back, the one rounded area of carving. Again, the imagery is strange; indeed, Gauguin provided the key to it in his title. A woman's head in profile glances sideways, meaningfully. Another woman gazes out inscrutably, with a warning gesture. The central figure turns away from us, moving wildly. These disjointed images are united by excited swirls of serpentine foliage. It is assuredly a mysterious work, bewitching and ambiguous.

But Gauguin could make totally three-dimensional sculpture. *Oviri* is a goddess of destruction. In a curious reversal, this voluptuous woman looms over a dead she-wolf, but it is the wolf that symbolizes maternity, while the sensuous female embodies death. All masses are simplified, drawing our eyes to the enormous hands, the high, firm breasts, and the death's-head mask of the face. So life and death meet in the eternal mystery of woman, primitive and terrifying.

Soyez Amoureuses et Vous Serez Heureuses (Be loving and you will be happy) 1889 Wood relief, painted 38¼ × 28¾ in (97.2 × 73 cm) Museum of Fine Arts, Boston, Arthur Tracy Cabot Fund

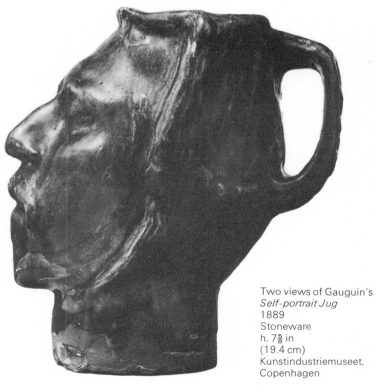

Two views of Gauguin's *Self-portrait Jug* 1889 Stoneware h. 7⅝ in (19.4 cm) Kunstindustriemuseet, Copenhagen

Picture Analysis:
Te Rereioa (The Dream)

Te Rereioa
(The Dream)
1897
Medium unavailable
$37\frac{1}{2} \times 51\frac{1}{4}$ in
(95.3 × 130.2 cm)
Courtauld Institute
Galleries,
London

It is extraordinary that, in the midst of physical and emotional torment, Gauguin should have produced *Te Rereioa*. No other painting of his is more free of doubt and turmoil, more assured and calm. It is imbued with a majestic silence, the silence of harmony and peace. Such an achievement is a tribute to the power of Gauguin's vision of Tahiti as the Paradise of the Age of Gold. Rarely can any artist create such a perfect realization of a vision, and we must examine the painting carefully to see how it was done.

The composition embodies several elements which Gauguin had used before: here they are employed with total mastery. The steeply tilted floor reminds us of his study of Cézanne and Japanese prints; it establishes a flat, abstract space in which the monumental, sculptural figures are anchored. One's eye is led out to the airy landscape beyond by the slanting line of floor and wall; at the same time, the space is stabilized and the eye drawn back to the centre of the picture by the horizontal mass of the cradle and the strong horizontal line below the doorway and far wall. The figures are literally framed by the light doorway and wall. Dark contour lines define and unite the dominant forms and shapes, while the formal geometry creates a space which is shallow and ambiguous, firmly contained without being claustrophobic.

The colours are truly those of the Golden Age. Gold touches everything: the glowing walls and floor, the bronze bodies and the rich landscape. It courses through the green

and brown shadows and the copper high-
lights, making even the darkest areas luminous. The close harmony of these colours
binds and unifies the diverse images; all are
invested with a barbaric splendour which no
reality can tarnish.

The imagery itself realizes Gauguin's high-
est ambitions: it is poetic and mysterious,
lyrical and enigmatic. Indeed, it is a poem
within a poem, a dream within a dream.
These handsome women embody the beauty
and the power of the tropics. They sit like
pagan idols of earthly bliss, self-possessed
and wholly at peace, keeping watch over the
sleeping child. Are they statues warming
into flesh, or the reverse? The sculpture on
the walls and cradle seems to tell the story of
their people: strange animals and primitive
gods and goddesses enact curious myths and
legends. And beyond the walls, a solitary
horseman moves through a shimmering
landscape. The women and child seem to
occupy a middle-ground between this vivid
land and the stylized drama of the sculpture.
They, themselves, are in the process of be-
coming a myth, balancing between past and
future, life and art.

Of this painting, Gauguin said, '*Te Rereioa,*
that is the title. Everything is dream-like in
this picture; is it the child, is it the mother, is
it the horseman on the track or better still is
it the dream of the painter! All that has
nothing to do with the painting, people will
say. Perhaps, but perhaps not.' Perhaps, in
truth, it is everyone's dream: the dream of a
time and place that may never have existed
in this world, but will always exist in man's
desires.

Detail of the horse and
rider from *Te Rereioa*

Detail of the wall sculpture
from *Te Rereioa*

Detail of the landscape
from *Te Rereioa*

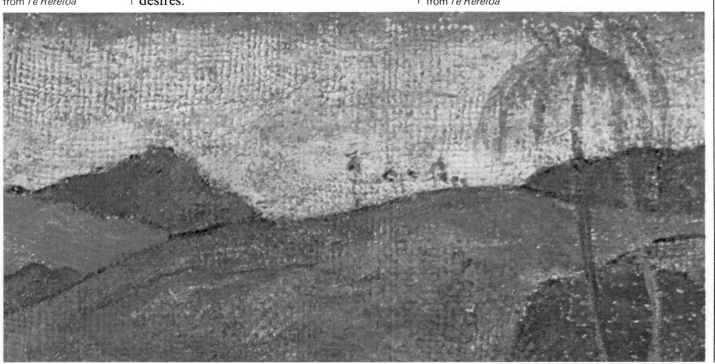

Biographical Outline

1848
June 7: Eugène-Henri-Paul Gauguin, son of Clovis and Aline, born in Paris.

1849
Gaugin family went to Peru; Clovis died *en route*.

1849-55
Gauguin family lived in Lima, Peru.

1855
The family returned to France. Lived at Orléans until 1859, then moved to Paris.

1865-67
Gauguin served in merchant marine.

1867
Death of Gauguin's mother, Aline, who appointed Gustave Arosa as guardian of her children.

1868-71
Gauguin served in French navy.

1871
With Gustave Arosa's help, he began work with the stockbroker, Bertin.
Met Schuffenecker at Bertin's. He became a good friend to Gauguin and encouraged him to paint.

1873
Began painting with the help of his guardian's daughter, Marguerite Arosa.
Married Mette Sophie Gad, a Danish governess.

1874
Birth of their first son, Emil.

*c.***1877**
Met Camille Pissarro (1831-1903), and began collecting Impressionist paintings.

1877
Birth of a daughter, Aline.

1879
Exhibited sculpture in fourth Impressionist exhibition.
Birth of a son, Clovis.
Worked with Pissarro.

1880
Exhibited at fifth Impressionist exhibition.

1881
Exhibited at sixth Impressionist exhibition.
Birth of a son, Jean.

1882
Helped organize seventh Impressionist exhibition.

1883
Left his job on the stock exchange.
Birth of a son, Paul (Pola).

1884
January: Moved to Rouen.
August: Mette went to Copenhagen with Aline and Paul.

Gauguin followed with the other children, and took up job as agent for Dillies and Co., manufacturers of tarpaulins.

1885
May: One-man exhibition at the Society of the Friends of Art, Copenhagen.
June: Returned to Paris with his son, Clovis.

1886
Exhibited in last Impressionist exhibition.
June: Went to Pont Aven in Brittany, where he met Emile Bernard (1868-1941).
October: Met Vincent Van Gogh (1853-90).

1887
April: Went to Panama, where he worked on the canal.
Moved to Martinique, then returned to France.

1888
February: Returned to Pont Aven.
October: One-man show at Goupils gallery, the branch run by Theo Van Gogh.
October 20-December 24: Stayed with Van Gogh in Arles at the request of Theo, Van Gogh's brother.
Painted *The Vision after the Sermon*.

1889
Exhibited with others at Café Volpini as *Groupe Impressioniste et Synthétiste*.
Returned to Pont Aven, and then went on to Le Pouldu.
Painted *La Belle Angèle* and *The Yellow Christ*.

1890
Stayed in Pont Aven and Le Pouldu for the summer.
Met Symbolist writers in Paris.

1891
Had a sale of paintings at Hôtel Drouot.
Visited his family in Copenhagen.
Went to Tahiti.

1892
Took thirteen-year-old Teha'amana as native wife.
Painted *Nafea Faaipoipo* (When are you to be married?) and *Ta Matete* (The Market).

1893
Returned to Paris.
Exhibited his Tahitian work at Galerie Durand-Ruel.
Began writing *Noa-Noa* with the Symbolist writer, Charles Morice.

1894
Took Annah the Javanese as his mistress.
Stayed at Le Pouldu with Annah.
Broke his leg in a fight with sailors.
Annah ransacked his Paris studio and deserted him.
Painted *Mahana no Atua* (The Day of God).

1895
Ill with syphilis.
Left Paris forever and returned to Tahiti. Settled at Punaauia.

1896
Took the fourteen-year-old Pahura as native wife, and became sicker and more poverty-stricken.
Painted *Nave Nave Mahana* (Days of Delight).

1897
Daughter Aline died.
Had to borrow money to move house and pay his debts.
Mette finally broke off correspondence with him.
Desperately depressed tried to commit suicide.
Painted *Nevermore, Te Rereioa* (The Dream) and *D'où Venons-Nous? Que Sommes-Nous? Où Allons-Nous?*

1898
Worked as a draughtsman in Public Works Department.
Painted *Faa Iheihe* (Decoration).

1899
Pahura bore a son, Emile.
Wrote articles for *Les Guêpes*, a periodical published in Papeete.
Published his own satirical periodical *Le Sourire* which continued to be produced until 1900.

1900
Active in local politics, and became editor of *Les Guêpes* to bring in some kind of income.
Art dealer Vollard began sending him a monthly allowance in return for his paintings. His standard of living improved slightly.

1901
In search of an even more primitive land, moved to the Marquesas Islands to Atuona and built himself a house, the 'House of Pleasure'.
Took a fourteen-year-old girl, Vaeho, as his mistress.

1902
Continued his activity in politics. Out of debt but refused to pay taxes and incited the natives to do the same.
Vaeho bore him a daughter.
Painted *Barbaric Tales*.

1902-03
Wrote *Avant et Après*. Unable to paint much because of worsening health and eyesight.

1903
Charged with libelling a *gendarme*; found guilty, sentenced to fine and three months' imprisonment.
Planned to go to Tahiti to appeal.
May 8: Died at Atuona.

Self-portrait c. 1893 Bronze bas-relief
$13\frac{1}{2} \times 14$ in (34.3 × 35.6 cm)
Art Institute, Chicago

Location of Major Works

Museums, galleries and collections in North America, and in the rest of the world where examples of Gauguin's work can be seen.

Boston
Museum of Fine Arts

Buffalo
Albright-Knox Art Gallery

Chicago
Art Institute

Cleveland
Museum of Art

Hawaii
Honolulu Academy of Arts

Indianapolis
John Herron Art Museum

Kansas City
Gallery of Art

Los Angeles
County Museum of Art

Minneapolis
Institute of Arts

New York
Metropolitan Museum of Art;
Museum of Modern Art

Northampton
Smith College Museum of Art

St Louis
City Art Museum

Washington D.C.
National Gallery of Art;
Phillips Gallery

West Palm Beach
Norton Gallery and School of Fine Art

Amsterdam
Rijksmuseum
Vincent van Gogh

Basle
Kunstmuseum

Brussels
Musées Royaux des Beaux-Arts

Copenhagen
Kunstindustriemuseet;
Ordrupgaard Museum

Edinburgh
National Gallery of Scotland

Essen
Folkwang Museum

Grenoble
Musée de Grenoble

Hamburg
Kunsthalle

Helsinki
Atheneum Museum

Leningrad
The Hermitage

London
Courtauld Institute Galleries;
Tate Gallery

Lyons
Musée des Beaux-Arts

Moscow
Pushkin Museum

Paris
Musée du Louvre;
Musée de Petit Palais

Prague
National Gallery

Rheims
Musée des Beaux-Arts

Sao Paulo
Museu de Arte

Stockholm
Nationalmuseum

Acknowledgements

The Publishers would like to thank all the museums, galleries and owners of private collections for permission to reproduce works in their care or possession. The caption to each illustration gives the location of the subject.

The photographs were provided by the following:
Cooper-Bridgeman Library, London 6; Courtauld Institute Galleries, London 2r, 9, 11b, 28, 29; Hamlyn Group Picture Library, London 4tl, tr, 7, 10, 11t, 18, 19t, b, 22, 23t, b, 27t, 31; Hinz Colorphoto, Basle 25t, b; Museum of Fine Arts, Boston 15t, b, 16; National Gallery of Art, Washington D.C. 1; Nationalmuseum, Stockholm 3b; Ole Woldbye, Copenhagen 27bl, br; Ordrupgaardsamlingen, Denmark 14; Photographie Giraudon, Paris 5, 20, 21, 32; Roger-Viollet Documentation Photographique, Paris 2l, 3t; Tom Scott, Edinburgh 8; Stedelijk Museum, Amsterdam 4b; Tate Gallery, London 12, 13; Whitney Collection, New York 24.

Still-life: Roses and Statuette c. 1890 28¾ × 21¼ in (73×54 cm) Musée des Beaux-Arts, Rheims